The Afterlife of Flowers

The Afterlife of Flowers

BY

JANIE FELDMAN GROSS

RUNNING PRESS
PHILADELPHIA · LONDON

9 8 7 6 5 4 3 2 1
Digit on the right indicates the number of this printing

Library of Congress Cataloging-in-Publication Number 98-68477

ISBN 0-7624-0570-8

Typography: Glypha, Bickley Script

This book may be ordered by mail from the publisher.
Please include $2.50 for postage and handling.
But try your bookstore first!

Running Press Book Publishers
125 South Twenty-second Street
Philadelphia, Pennsylvania 19103-4399

Visit us on the web!
www.runningpress.com

To my mother,

for

showing me

my first flower.

Acknowledgments

I am eternally grateful to my dear friend, Charles Santore, for suggesting that I write and design a book featuring my pressed flower images—and Olenka Santore, for her confidence and wisdom.

My deep appreciation to those who helped, especially—

My talented editor, Caroline Tiger, for her gentle guidance and support.

The special people at Running Press, for instantly believing in my book and for making it a reality.

Beverly Schaeffer of Schaeffer Flowers, for allowing me to press flowers from her extraordinary cutting gardens.

Louis Greene, for his generous technological assistance.

My daughters, Toby and Julie, for constantly inspiring and amazing me.

My husband, Peter, who really made this book with me and who continually fortifies me with his encouragement, patience, and kindness.

In loving memory
of my father,
who provided music for my soul.

Contents

INTRODUCTION

*P*ressed flowers have been discussed and photographed in numerous books and publications. There are volumes on techniques and ideas for the creative application of the successfully pressed material. Often, pressed material is used for collages and for detailed compositions comprised of a mixture of many different plants.

It occurred to me that each pressed flower is so uniquely beautiful that it deserves to be enlarged and viewed individually in order to fully appreciate the "afterlife," which occurs as a result of pressing and drying. The images I create highlight the singularity of each dried blossom.

I set out to press the flowers the moment I pick them from the garden. In doing so I have developed a passion for the entire process of harvesting, pressing, and rediscovering.

After the lifelines (stem and water supply) have been cut and the flowers have been placed into the press, the magic begins. Reopening the presses after waiting the appropriate drying time sets my heart racing with wonder. What were once multidimensional, complex structures transform into compressed, delicate forms which reveal changed personalities. The fragility of these diaphanous shapes is rivaled only by butterfly wings. One merely has to breathe the wrong way and a bunch of petals take flight!

Unlike the goal of certain pressers—to achieve perfect color retention and shape—I constantly delight in the fading and imperfections that occur. This enthusiasm is akin to an appreciation for the warm, rich patina of painted antique furniture and a fondness for the textural quality and luminosity of delicate fabrics and handmade papers.

The magnified images that follow provide an intimate view of flowers that are ordinarily too small to scrutinize. Each flower is accompanied by comments taken from my garden journal, inspired by the moment of discovery when I first reopen the presses. Surprisingly, each one takes on a whole new life as a mystical graphic impression. In order to maintain that mystique, the names do not always accompany the flowers. Flower identification can be found at the end of the book.

Best of all, I have found a way to revisit the garden in winter. As I gaze out my studio window at the blank flower beds of January, all I have to do is open my drawer full of pressed flowers from last spring, summer, and fall, and I can almost feel the warm sunshine on the back of my neck.

J.F.G.

The

stem

is like the

skater's arms.

It gives the flower "life"

just as gesturing arms exemplify

the spirit of the heart.

Literally and figuratively,

the stem provides

life to the flower.

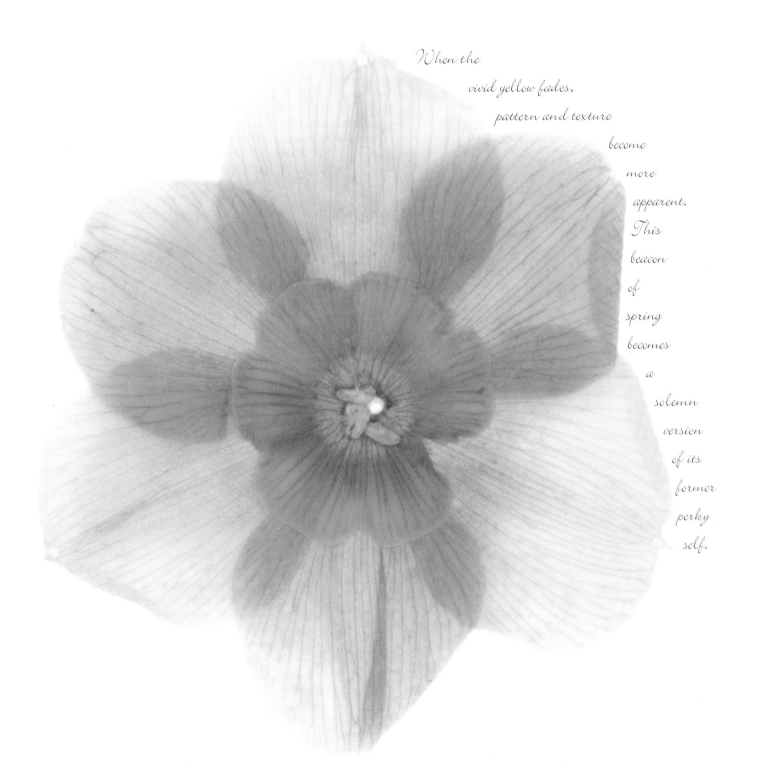

When the
vivid yellow fades,
pattern and texture
become
more
apparent.
This
beacon
of
spring
becomes
a
solemn
version
of its
former
perky
self.

Some perennials are so profusely covered with blooms, it's easy to miss the dramatic simplicity of each singular flower until one is selected for pressing. This looks like a burst of sunshine atop a fine blade of grass.

Although

the elevated stamen

of this flower

is remarkable.

I had to remove it

for pressing.

The drying time

was extremely long

due to

the quantity of

moisture.

The result

speaks for itself.

By pressing a flower
with its stem
attached,
it appears as if
it is still growing.

By including

the young buds,
a sense of
immortality
is established.

Originally cup-shaped, there is a striking
difference when flattened.
I would never have known
that each petal is a
perfectly shaped heart.
The yellow is as
brilliant as the day
it was picked.

These diaphanous petals exemplify the mottled appearance I find so appealing.

Usually hidden from view,
the undersides of flowers reveal their own delicate symmetry when flattened by pressing.

Even
though
this
paper-thin
bud
lost
all of its
original color,
it maintains a
strong personality
and
an intriguing
sense
of dimension.

Holding onto
its color
for dear life
and
looking like
it was
dipped
ever so
carefully
into
indigo dye;
its pigment
"bleeds" —
the same way
ink
would
respond to
rice
paper.

The books say

that flowers

containing a lot

of moisture will

not press or dry

successfully.

Here is proof

that certain

beauty would go

undiscovered

without the

experimentation

prompted by

curiosity.

There are no

limitations

when merging

nature with

creativity.

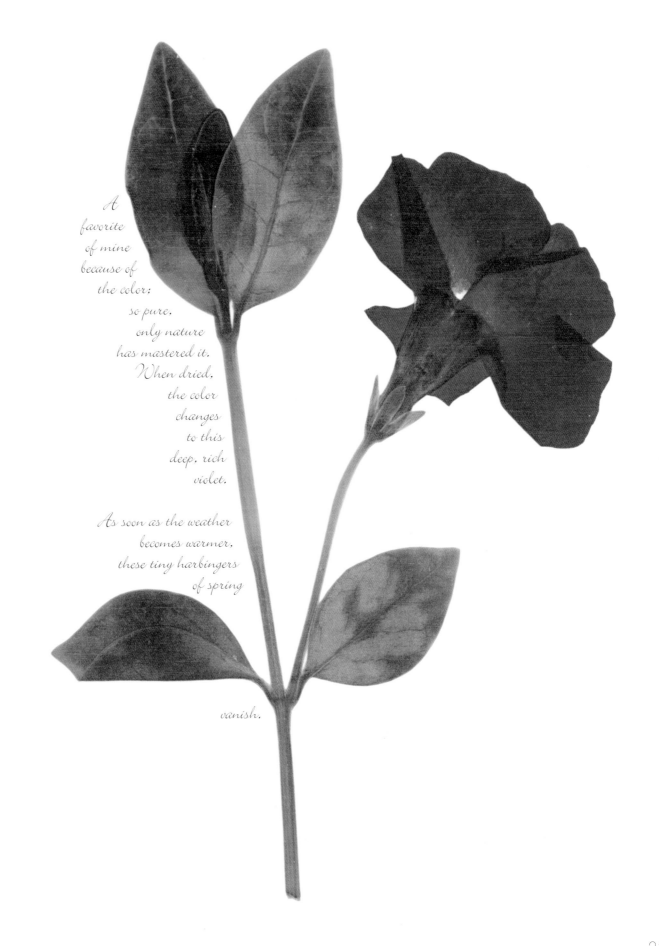

A
favorite
of mine
because of
the color;
so pure,
only nature
has mastered it.
When dried,
the color
changes
to this
deep, rich
violet.

As soon as the weather
becomes warmer,
these tiny harbingers
of spring

vanish.

Nature shows no favoritism.
She lines the roadsides
with abundant lace
for everyone, rich or poor.
To ensure my own
abundant supply,
I scatter seeds
in the fall
in order
to reap
the benefits
the following
summer.

Ideal
for
adding
rhythm
to
floral
arrangements
by cutting
fresh,
or
allowing
to dry
to a pale amber.

Enlarging
the
pressed flowers
is quite different from
using a microscope, because one sees
the entire image at once rather than in sections. This introduces the startling
contrasts of colors, shapes, and textures.

I

have

always

marveled

at

the

total

simplicity

and

smoothness.

The
parts
are
just
as
magnificent
as the
whole.

Pressing the petals
separately
reveals so much
about
the architecture
of that flower.

A
garden
with
tulips
represents
a
gardener
with
optimism.

I can tolerate the
numbness
of my fingers in the
autumn soil
because
my heart is warm
with the secret
that is
the promise of spring.

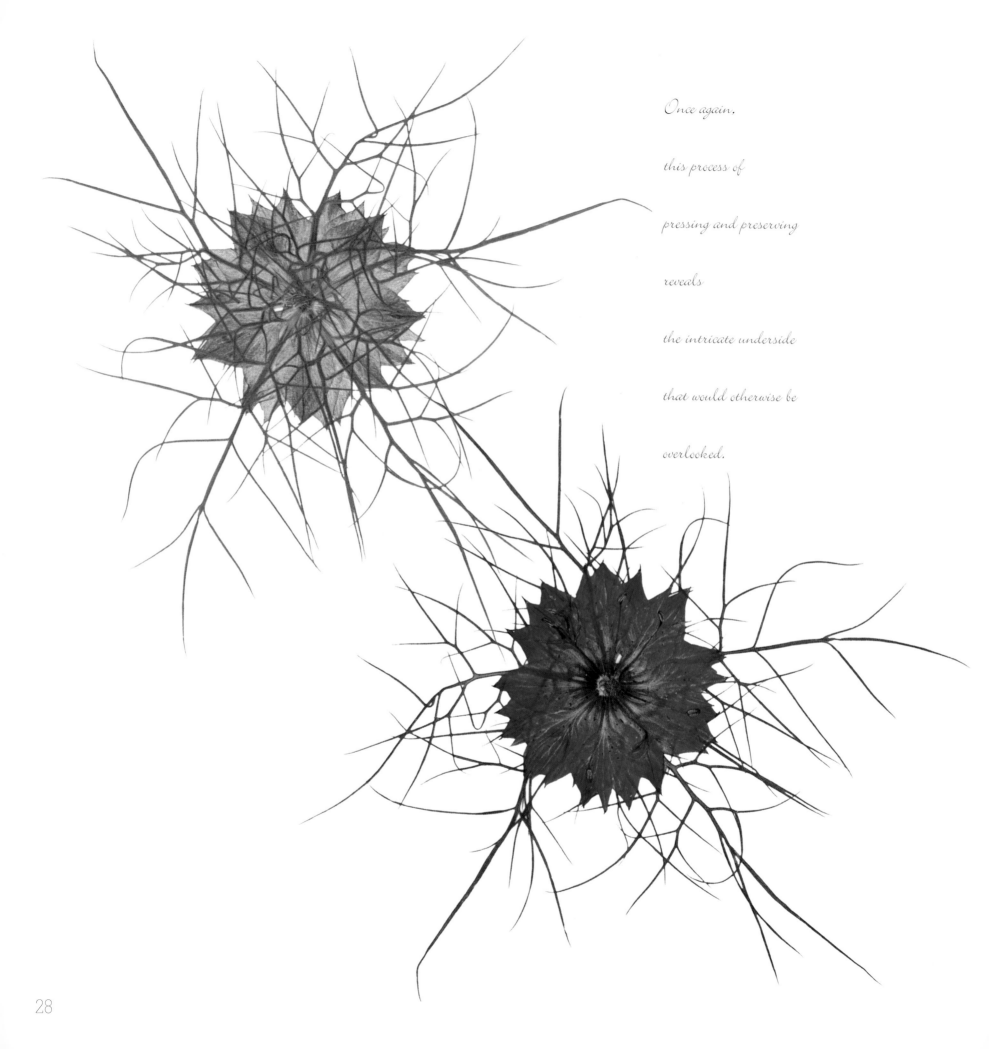

Once again,

this process of

pressing and preserving

reveals

the intricate underside

that would otherwise be

overlooked.

Talk about having it all:

texture, delicacy, splendid color,

and superb longevity for

both cutting and pressing.

The seedpods are

masterful packages

for the tiny seeds that

propagate so easily

when

scattered about.

I thought

this flower

would never press

due to the thickness of its center,

but, because my husband, Peter, bought it

for me with the hopes of it becoming

part of this collection,

I had to try it.

And sure enough,

as always,

love endures!

Certain things

are best left

unexplained.

Certain images evoke certain emotions—
this one leaves me speechless.

"Is that a flower?" you ask.

Is it possible that
the cell-like splotches
tell of the curative
powers within?

Speculation fuels the imagination.

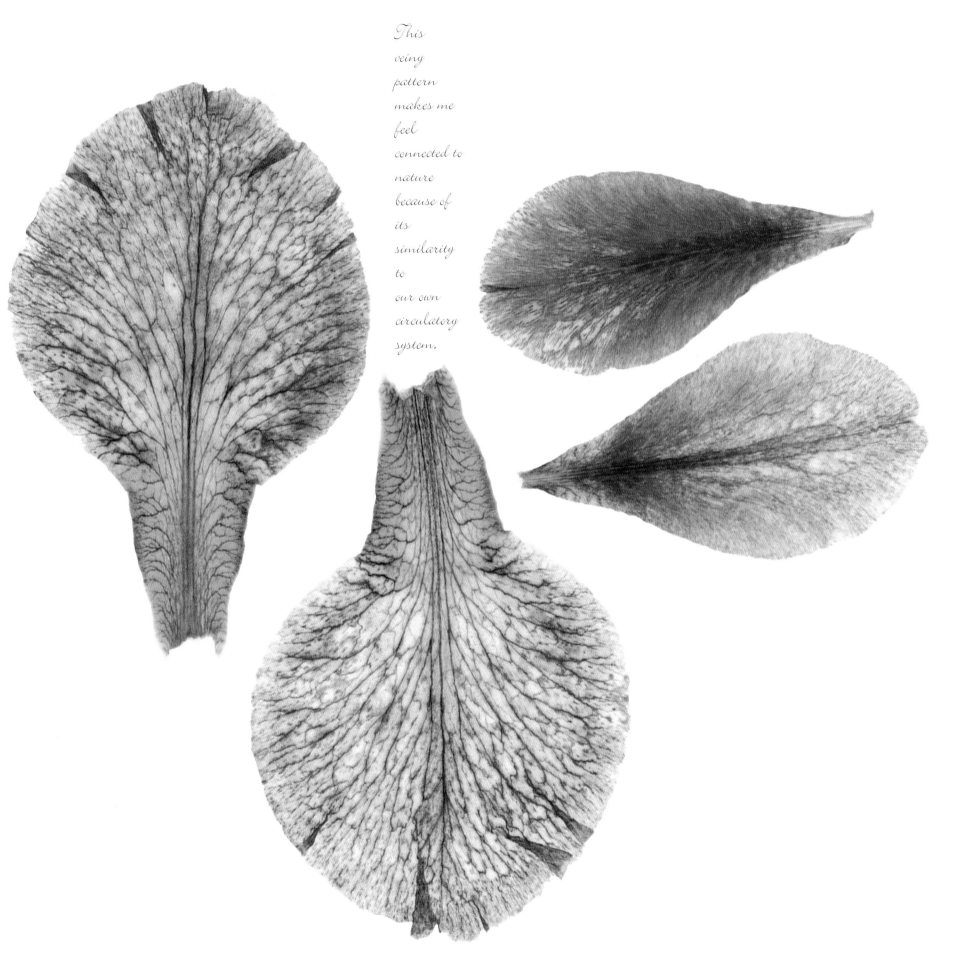

This
veing
pattern
makes me
feel
connected to
nature
because of
its
similarity
to
our own
circulatory
system.

As a graphic designer
I will always see the power of related objects . . .

. . . juxtaposed.

Is this a
reflection
of my
happy face
looking at
the first sign
of spring?
Or
do they
just know
we need
cheering up
after
the dreariness
of winter?

Now that science has contributed a winter variety of this popular annual, who will be the first to smile when spring returns?

It amazes me how familiar faces emanate such rare beauty.
The modest treasures of our earth must not be
taken for granted.

Variations on a theme.

Again and again, the art of

pressing forces me to analyze each flower

and break it down into parts,

such as this floret,

which is

a small part

of a very

familiar

summer

flower.

Viewing the entire stem

with its flowers attached provides valuable information for identification purposes.

Artistic license allows me to straighten an otherwise floppy specimen.
It's positively inspiring to observe one type of flower
from varying perspectives.

If this were an abstract painting,

we'd say that the small yellow crescent shapes are strategically placed

on the pink background to create a sense of movement. Is it the art of nature or the nature of art?

Both

artists

and

scientists

benefit

from

the

deeper

understanding

that

dissection

provides.

I've always enjoyed viewing familiar objects

out of context.

The gesture is everything—

in dance

and

in flower arranging.

Previously part of
a tightly clustered
stalk,
this tiny
masterpiece
stands proudly
alone.

All
dressed up in
a
funky
little hat and
fitted coat.

waiting
to
show off
its
extravagant
attire . . .

. . . the drama unfolds.

We

can't

always

predict

the

beauty . . .

. . . that lies within.

Formerly

contained

in snowball clusters

it's

refreshing

to experience

each individual floret . . .

. . . in motion.

Viewing a single enlarged petal enhances your perception of flowers forever.

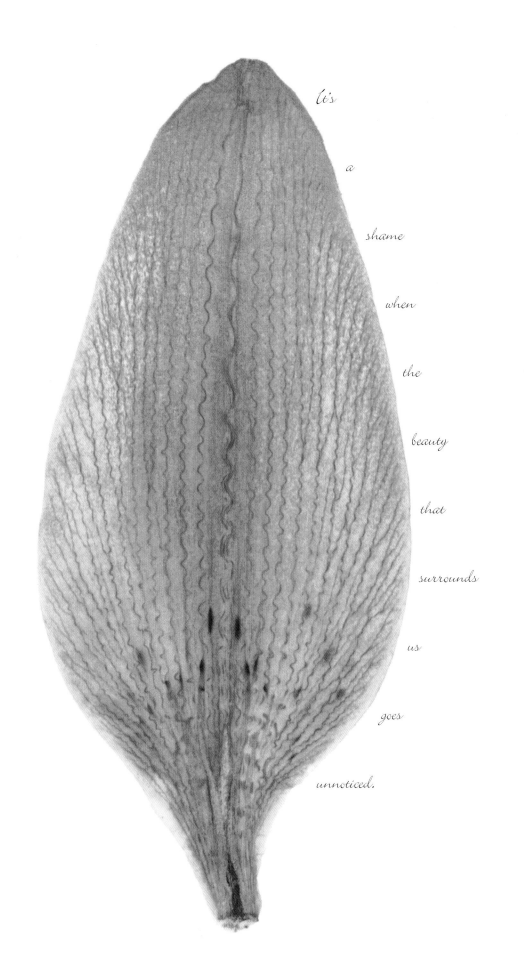

It's

a

shame

when

the

beauty

that

surrounds

us

goes

unnoticed.

It's hard to believe how many versions of
five-pointed stars
exist.

It's
such
a
thrill
to
introduce
tropical
flowers
to a
northern
garden.

Occasionally the eyes need to rest on white space to enable the appreciation of . . .

. . . form and structure.

There are times

when we say,

"This can't be real!"

It is then that we question,

what *is* real?

Examining

these two flowers

side by side

illuminates

the limitless

potential

of

creativity.

Often
pooh-poohed
by
elite gardeners,
these are
always
welcome guests
in
my garden.

Reaching toward the millennium.

This hardy perennial has continued to bloom in my garden for five months in full sun—

a gardener's dream!

Such

a

nice

addition

to the

perennial

border

since

it

provides

linear motion,

great color,

and

an

added

feature—

fragrance.

A Stop sign for bees—

imagine
a
town
with
one
on
every corner.

Evoking images of butterflies, Rorschach ink,

and

Japanese

paint-

brushes,

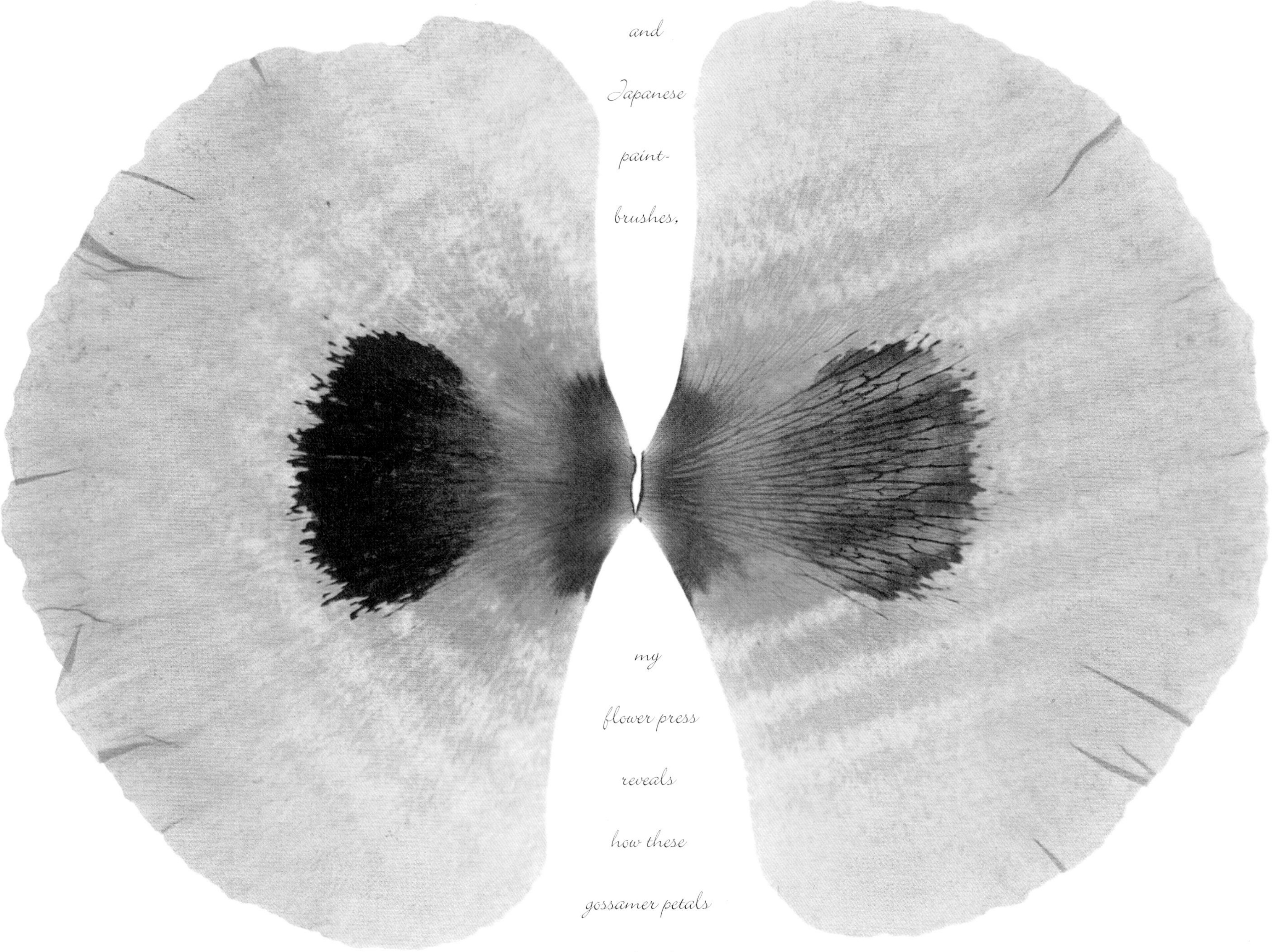

my

flower press

reveals

how these

gossamer petals

have faded in color, but not in spirit.

I'm

constantly

intrigued

by

how

shapes

elicit

sensations.

I

can

feel

the

dynamic

energy

of the

pointy

petals

and

chaotic

center

in

contrast

to . . .

. . . the serenity of rounded petals and perfect symmetry.

Perhaps flowers represent the larger components of our immense universe. With a little imagination this could be a Native American symbol for the sun.

Just add wind and wedding bells.

The smallest yellow flower can brighten up the dullest day.

It's no wonder the Japanese beetle selects this bed for mating. It presents an air of titillation.

Again
and
again
it's
difficult
to
believe
that
something
so
common
can
become
perfectly
regal
depending
on
how
it
is
perceived.

The petals become transparent
when pressed and dried, rendering a delightful layered, tissue-paper-like quality.

There are very few true orange-red flowers, so it is exciting to find out that this one maintains its color extremely well after pressing and drying.

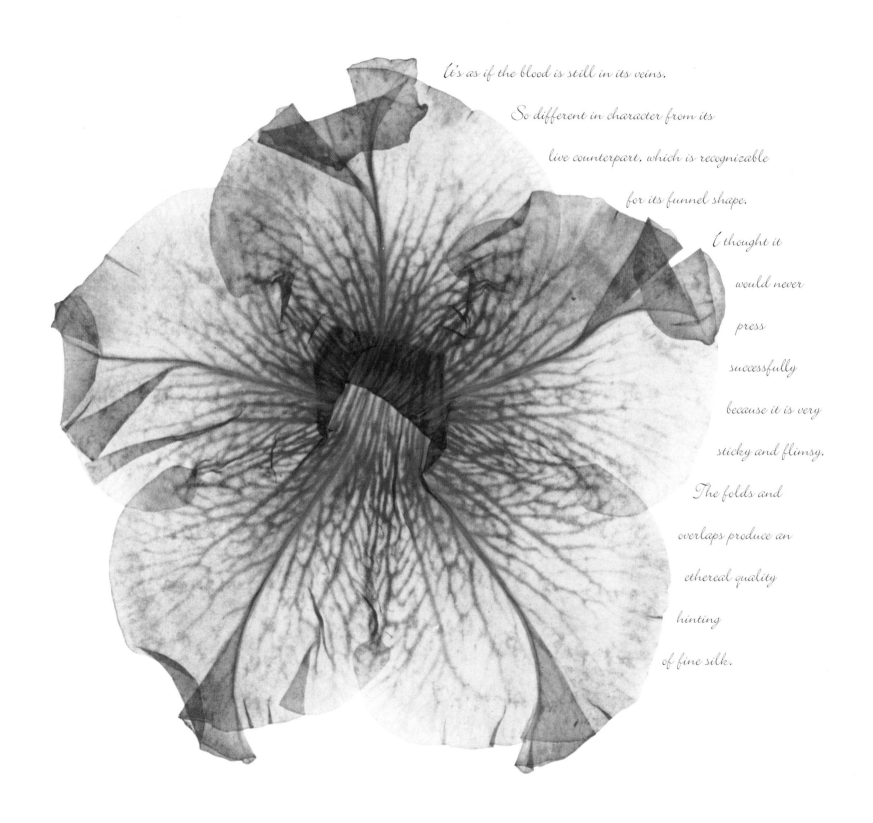

It's as if the blood is still in its veins.

So different in character from its

live counterpart, which is recognizable

for its funnel shape.

I thought it

would never

press

successfully

because it is very

sticky and flimsy.

The folds and

overlaps produce an

ethereal quality

hinting

of fine silk.

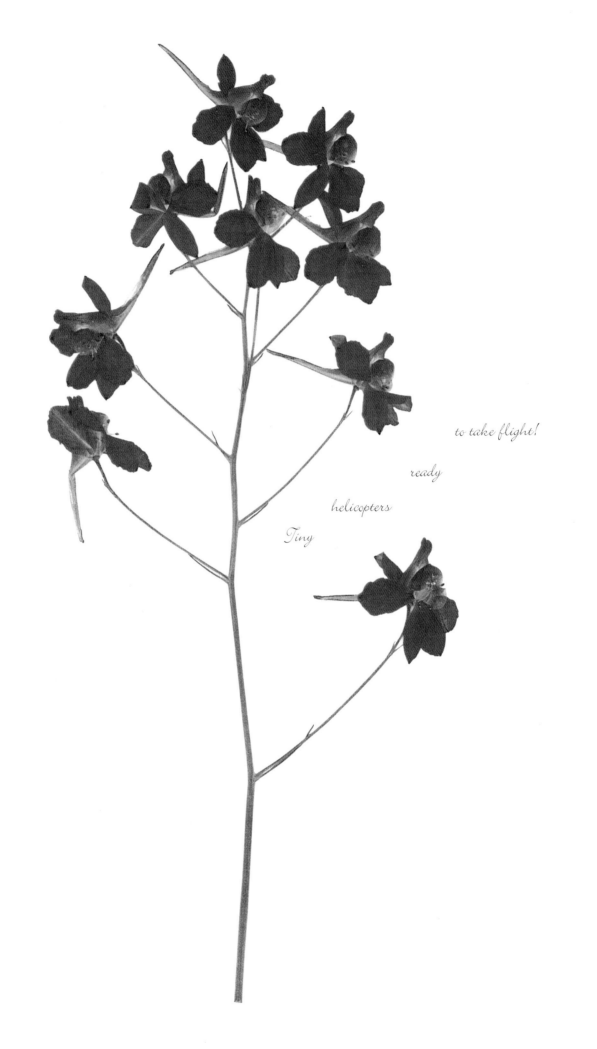

Tiny
helicopters
ready
to take flight!

Symmetry occurs   *over and over again.*

Void

of

their

intense

colors,

it's

easy

to

savor

the

structural

elegance.

It's fascinating to study

the similarities

and differences

within families.

One sprig becomes a tree for the flower presser.

You have to

touch

this flower

to believe it!

Since

baby blue

is so rare in eyes and flowers,

each encounter is as exciting as the first.

It is always
a challenge
to create
a sense of motion
with
perfectly flat
images.

Nature

constantly

reinvents . . .

. . . the pinwheel.

Identification

Front cover
Cosmos
flower width: 2 inches

Page 10
Johnson's Blue Geranium
flower width: 1.5–2 inches

Page 11
Jonquil
flower width: 2 inches

Page 12
Coreopsis Moonbeam
flower width: 1 inch

Page 13
Passion Flower
flower width: 2 inches

Page 14
Perennial Geranium
flower width: .5–1 inch

Page 15
Sundrops
flower width: 1.5 inches

Pages 16–17
Cosmos
flower width: 2 inches

Pages 18–19
Balloon Flower
flower width: 2–3 inches

Page 20
Impatiens
flower width: 1–2 inches

Page 21
Periwinkle
flower width: .5–1 inch

Page 22
Queen Anne's Lace
flower width: 2–2.5 inches

Page 23
Flowering Dogwood
flower width: 2 inches

Page 24
Tulip
flower width: 2–2.5 inches

Page 25
Tulip petals
petal width: 2 inches

Page 26
Tulips
flower width: 1.5 inches

Measurement denotes size of actual flower.

Page 27
Tulip
flower width: 3 inches

Pages 34–35
Alstroemeria
flower width: 2 inches

Page 28
Love-in-a-mist
flower width: 1.5 inches

Pages 36–37
Pansies
flower width: 1.5 inches

Page 29
Love-in-a-mist
flower width: 1.5 inches

Page 38
Johnny-jump-ups
flower width: 1 inch

Page 30
Gerbera
flower width: 2.5 inches

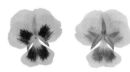

Page 39
Viola
flower width: 1.5 inches

Page 31
Daffodil
flower width: 2 inches

Page 40
Annual Geranium (individual floret)
flower width: 1 inch

Page 32
Foxglove
flower width: 1.5 inches

Page 41
Delphinium
flower width: 1 inch

Page 33
Iris petals
petal widths: 1–1.5 inches

Page 42
Primrose
flower width: 1.25 inches

Page 43
Primrose
flower width: 2 inches

Page 44
Hosta
flower width: 1 inch

Pages 52–53
Hydrangea (individual floret)
floret width: 1 inch

Page 45
Hosta
flower width: 1 inch

Page 54
Clematis petal
petal width: 2 inch

Page 46
Larkspur
flower width: 1 inch

Page 55
Clematis petal
petal width: 2 inches

Page 47
Larkspur (individual floret)
floret width: 1 inch

Page 56
Mallow
flower width: 2.5 inches

Page 48
Hibiscus
flower width: 3 inches

Page 57
Mandevilla
flower width: 2.5–3 inches

Page 49
Hibiscus
flower width: 3 inches

Pages 58–59
Garden Pink
flower width: 1 inch

Page 50
Clematis
bud length: 1.5 inches

Page 60
Gazania
flower width: 1.5 inches

Page 51
Clematis
flower width: 2.5 inches

Page 61
Chrysanthemum
flower width: 2 inches

Measurement denotes size of actual flower.

Identification

Page 62
Marigold
flower width: 1 inch

Page 63 and back cover
Cupid's Dart
flower width: 1 inch

Page 64
Salvia
flower stalk length: 4–5 inches

Page 65
Gazania
flower width: 1.5 inches

Page 66
Painted Tongue
flower width: 1.5 inches

Page 67
Poppy petals
petal width: 3 inches

Page 68
Stokes' Aster
flower width: 2 inches

Page 69
Pincushion Flower
flower width: 1.5 inches

Page 70
Blanket flower
flower width: 1.5 inches

Page 71
petals of Zinnia, Blanket flower, and
Orange Coneflower
petal widths: 1–1.5 inches

Page 72
Loosestrife
flower width: .5 inch

Page 73
Zinnia
flower width: 1.5 inches

Page 74
Rose
flower width: 2 inches

Page 75
Crown Vetch
flower width: .5–1 inch

Page 76
Phlox
flower width: 1.5 inches

Page 77
Cosmos
flower width: 1.5 inches

Page 78
Petunia
flower width: 2–3 inches

Page 84
Cockscomb
flower width: 1.5 inches

Page 79
Larkspur
flower width: .5 inch

Page 85
Delphinium (individual floret)
floret width: 1 inch

Page 80
Clematis
flower width: 2.5 inches

Page 86
Evening Primrose
flower width: 2.5 inches

Page 81
Fuchsia
flower width: 1 inch

Page 87
Bellflower
flower width: 1 inch

Page 82
Cosmos
flower width: 2.5 inches

Page 88
Cosmos
flower width: 2 inches

Page 83
Coral Bells
flower width: .5 inch

Page 89
Hibiscus
flower width: 2.5 inches

Measurement denotes size of actual flower.

Afterword

"Good things come in small packages."

I've been listening to these words since I was a young girl due

to my 5-foot 1-inch frame. The same words also apply to flowers. After

looking at this book, it may be difficult to think of flowers as "small,"

not only because the images are so magnified, but also because you

have encountered their souls. Some change more dramatically than

others, but all acquire a new guise. My hope is that as you return to

the "real" world you will not be deceived by size, now that you've seen

the beauty and potential that exist within nature's tiny gems.

J.F.G.